I Walk The Fens

by

Susan Sansby

Copyright © 2023 Susan Sansby

ISBN: 9781916981126

All rights reserved, including the right to reproduce this book, or portions thereof in any form. No part of this text may be reproduced, transmitted, downloaded, decompiled, reverse engineered, or stored, in any form or introduced into any information storage and retrieval system, in any form or by any means, whether electronic or mechanical without the express written permission of the author.

Foreword

Susan moved to Ely in her 70's and was inspired by her surroundings to write this collection of poems. Although written late in life they display a freshness and spontaneity of the new life Susan had chosen for herself. A freshness and spontaneity of pleasures newly discovered and of thoughts and feelings re-discovered. New beginnings and reflections on the past.

Editor's Note and Acknowledgements

This edition is based on performance versions. I have arranged the poems by related subject matter, although that is a very loose arrangement. Places, Moments of Reflection and Observations from the past. They are not published in chronological order but rather by related content. My thanks to the organisers of Fenspeak at the Babylon Gallery, Ely, Cambridgeshire where I had the privilege to perform these works on their 'Open Mike' nights which helped so much in the preparation of this published version.

I apologise in advance for any errors or omissions which are entirely my own

Bruce
Editor

CONTENTS

Wicken Fen

Croyland

Flag Fen

Anglesey Abbey in Autumn

Reflecting on the Great River Ouse at Ely

The Blackbird

Dream

Jewels

A Path to Peace

The Working Horse

Wicken Fen

I walk the Fen,

Surrounded by immediate silence, save for a slight swish of reeds,

And a pheasant, startled, lifts itself into a hurried heavy, low flying escape.

I enter the hide.

Sneakily looking out of wooden narrow windows from a hard bench.

An uninvited visitor – a trespasser –

A trespasser transformed, led into unexpected pause by the birds.

Inexplicable yet distinct, comes this welcome lull from life

Into goldfinch, chaffinch, dunnock and bullfinch land.

Where have they been? – for so long unseen

and now together, surprising me.

They give generously as they zoom, lurch and balance so gently.

Never misjudging a twig.

Never clumsy or scrabbling but performing their spontaneous aerobatics.

A dance of perfection.

I.

A spy.

A thief, assuming a selfish right to impose and take from them, for my own mindful benefit.

I wonder briefly – am I watched? Does some unknown take from me as I take from them?

In these rich moments and with this thought, the world comes to a halt.

It stops.

On hold,

Merging into a taking and giving which has a balanced rhythmn.

Motionless, and with mind in limbo, for a time self-actualised, free and complete.

The squirrel jumps!

Suddenly and violently

The spell is broken.

Pheasant like they scurry and scatter in twittering panic.

I walk on. No longer a spy but a part of where I belong.

This is the gift of the Fens on a late afternoon in April.

Croyland

(Reflecting on Crowland Abbey)

In the Fens of England.

Lofty Ely soars. Mightily. Skyward,

Where Regal Peregrines nest

 In her tall impersonal towers.

A statement of power

from William the Norman

In his bid to subdue the rebel Fen landers.

And also – as the crow flies - North West,

Long before Ely's Ship existed,

Croyland Abbey sits.

Silently pointing her stone finger to the ever- changing skies

Which lie above.

Not to subdue – but to embrace

All who come modestly – and in Grace,

In memory of Guthlac, her Saint.

Where habited Monks, tended the sick

and lived piously,

defending their way of life,

defying poverty, damp and danger.

Modestly.

She sits.

Her plain crows fly and strut.

Less proud than Ely Falcons, but
She is Confident,

Dignified.

Proclaiming without a sound

That God sits, persists, in this mystical land's mists.

In smaller structures.

The remains of the Abbey,

Treasure to all who know her,

Named for the softness of the low- lying land on which she stands.

Emanates calm.

Once mired in mud and marsh.

Drawing pilgrims to that same flat island

Where Guthlac crossed,

Floating,

By boat, in six hundred and ninety-nine,

And yet she still speaks to you.
Take time to hear.
No grandeur here,
No power here,
No pomp in her message.
Benedictine simplicity.
A continuing constant of faith and peace.

Saunter along quiet Croyland lanes,
And touch them as would Saxons do
And Danes and Normans too.
And later as Parliamentarians and Royalists who
Battled,
Beside and within her.

An earthquake struck!
The Abbey stood,
Stuck.
Glued into the damp lands.
Shaken not destroyed.
By Luck?
Or Saintly design
She resists atmospheric and physical decline.

Her essential symbol?
the history enacted around her,
Intact.
Famed names have flitted into her walls and settled there for all
Time.
Or floated out again accompanied by numerous unknowns.

In the symbol that remains,
A turbulent history proclaims, continuous survival.
An unbroken, profoundly meaningful existence of
A developing culture,
Culminating under big skies
In the Fenland peace of today.

Carved into her façade are
William and Mathilda.
Hereward, the fighter,
Who, legend says, haunts Bourne still,
He too was drawn
between Ely and Croyland.
Fighting the cause of freedom.

Where now is the Wake?
His bones; hidden, assimilated in her stones
For peaceful eternity?

Were Croyland to crumble the Fens would be less.
Lost in stumbling, meaningless,
nothingness.
To lose the view of her through tall blocks and buildings
Swamping her structure,
pressing in close,
taking away,
diminishing,
obliterating
Both a Faith and
The heart of Fen spirit.

So go!
While you can.
Cross, that three cornered bridge!
Pause.
Gaze on Christ's image
as he sits there.
Water and marsh long gone.

Listen!

Stand in ageless space.

Walk ancient Croyland.

Brush senses against your face,
In the breezes that gently blow.

Treasure this vibrantly sacred space.

Feel the tangible essence,
That is the legacy of the Fens.

Preserve it for those who come humbly - come seeking.

For the sake of those who came before.

For they still,

Speak here.

Flag Fen

Diminished images from the Flag Fen Basin
Survive, and rise up to face the present day.
Eerily,
they stand before us having lain hidden
for thousands of years.

The sprayed causeway wood, is perpetually wettened.
Sitting,
almost in a modern shrine setting.
What was open for its population to use -
Is now covered,
No less sacred.
Artistic interpretations of the seasons surround it,
with written suggestions to prompt us
into thinking, "what was it like?"
to be a bronze age fenlander, in 3,500 BC.

I see,
In this Prehistory – the source of our own ritualistic behaviours.
Whilst we lay flowers for the dead
And have prayers said
For any number of reasons,

Visible here is true reverence and respect for the environment.

In the use of flag fen

Our ritual now is a drive on the part of the few

to preserve just a fraction of

This wonderful flat fenland history, with its wide skies,

that even I

after so many years can never see enough of.

Not so strange then that our ancient ancestors

Worshipped the glorious nature around them,

Made their **Gods** of water, sky, sun and moon.

and built

this long causeway – with its central platform,

A multi-purpose walk.

Straight from end to end, and

on route they might pause to watch their ritual offerings sink into the water.

Was this a toll for crossing

Or a safety offering en route?

And more importantly how could they be

so sure no other mortal

will take, and make off with their offerings?

What does this peep through an ancient doorway say to us today?

Many just glimpse it and walk away,

far more interested in getting to the tea hut.

But, make no haste to do that –

this long flat, space

has much to relate, even to the casual visitor.

Clearly one long path was enough to go through from end to end with flocks and family,

To get to a place of bartering and exchange

on all manner of human life.

One long path was enough for a warrior to walk or patrol.

Unhindered,

to the central platform and

Offer his sword – broken perhaps after battle.

Did he have a new one and was giving thanks for the old

as he rose through the ranks from many victories?

This could be the bronze age motorway

Embracing all human need.

Today we see different kinds of motorway, less rich, less human.

No belief and ritual in play beside and under its path.

Just a driving desire to get 'somewhere'.

The flag iris wave on the fen.
Nearby, plastic bags
filled with modern waste, are thoughtlessly dumped
Amidst the clumps, of their yellow heads in the dykes.
Bags thrown there,
by a Roman Road, where legionaries once tramped –
in heavy armour,
Their main motorway more cramped, but just as straight.
No wood for them.
Theirs is more durable of brick and pebble,
It needs no water to preserve it.
Their rituals were transportable, on the move –
not fixed to a sacred space.
Place and space are simply to be conquered
In barbarian, tribal, wild Britannia.

Boudicca is so close here -
by the Roman Road.
See her in her chariot in your mind's eye,
As we now walk these spaces
Never giving a thought, to the layers of life
that brought us to where we are,
laying the minimum foundations of preservation.

This layer, does not preserve much.
It uses and disposes.
How many layers will follow that deserve preserving -
As we move on from the present day?
Not many – everything in this layer is disposable and throwaway.
Just like the plastic bags, that lie by the yellow irises, in Flag Fen.

Anglesey Abbey in Autumn

Strikingly, Suddenly -
An avenue appears of
Tall and comforting colours that rise high ahead
and beside
in straight and perfectly placed positions and lines.
Swirling, curling, upwards
In shapely cone-like manner
Pointing loftily,
Spiking determinedly
to the clouds and skies above.

Colours displayed, sprayed,
Randomly arrayed.
Pleasing and easing
to tired eyes
after the sun strain
that blazed, for days, in '22;
'The Summer of Discomfort'
When all around
green turned to brown and died.
Heading, draining skin and plants,
Almost to a point of no return.

Yet here they are
Recovered.
For reflecting walkers to
Float by, along and upon
Weaving, gliding
through the paths of vibrant shades
that lay; before, behind, above and besides.
edging the glades, where statues stand squirrelled away in their leafy hidey holes.

Yellow, mustard, orange.
Pink, fuchsia, Green,
lime, privet, cedar dark and sage,
plum light and damson red and faded green,
khaki and jade.
Brown, copper, bronze and gold,
The Pheasant stands, in the morning light
flashing reds, rusts and whites
to behold.
In the midst of this panorama
of soft and warming hues
that fall surrounding and enfolding
those who amble through,
cradled by, and in, the colours of Autumn
at Anglesey Abbey.

All is damp and Moist today,

rain drenched at last from morning drizzle,

The trees are revived,

Nourished, hydrated, alive!

A Mini Eden of indescribably warmth.

Fluttering, falling leaves float down to the path

For feet to press or rest upon,

A feast and a flourish

That sits in the mind's eye long after

The path is gone, and the walk is over.

Inside the house Constable's shades and splash

Cannot compare

With the brush and dashing flash canvas, of undisturbed nature outside.

The eternal startling glare of reds and greens, lashes the view still

In a dramatic scene,

of everchanging colours,

the hue of soft dreams.

Shimmering showers of light, cascade from above
A twinkle and sheen of white,
There is no mental struggle
In beholding 'this' picture for
The palette of nature simply 'is';
It is 'There'.
It is 'Seen'.
For the thoughtful walker
To ponder upon.
Unable to avoid.
In warm mood
Wrapped in scarf, hat and gloves
A constant evolving collage,
Presses gently and firmly upon us
Urging its rich deep verdant smells
and bright contrasting sights into our senses
Reviving us in kind.
A frieze of living panoramic art
Temporary – until Winter arrives.
When the colours die and dry.
Until Spring revives,
their primary state again.

Reflecting on the River Great Ouse at Ely

Fast swirling,
Flushing, flurrying peaks and troughs.
Floods the wet writhing water
within the firm winding banks,
Built to withstand repetitive, relentless force,
Time and time again
Day by day
With no remorse, or respite.

So the old river rushes,
Runs, skurries,
relentlessly rippling, receding
Returning at will.
Rise of the tide, fall of the tide, waves lazily wandering,
Meandering, lingering, gliding,
Never ever still,
Ripples taking wing, distorting, flurrying
Flying.
Away
To distant horizons!

Forceful, fluent,
threatening with menace
flows the fast current with feisty force,
Demanding its freedom.
Continued and aimless
going and flowing
On chosen course -
The natural phenomena of the river
rules supreme, in glistening sheen -
Defiant to change.

Yet all around it changes
Dramatic and bold.
The people, the landscape, the weather, the old
What is new
Starts and departs
Leaving the city river
To flow
At its heart.

On its way,
Uninterrupted,
Not swayed
To deviate
Sustaining life, allowing life,
Giving peace to the aimless wanderer
On the bank.
Silently watching.

The Blackbird

Dinosaur like,

They fight

 For supremacy of the garden.

A running hop,

Along the top, of the long back garden fence.

Not a stumble as they rumble, headlong

Along the narrow top rail.

Falling and flumping midway, almost to the ground.

Then, spreading their spindly bony feathered wings, umbrella like and wide

Rising and falling simultaneously together,

They lock!

Frenzied; Ferocious.

Suspended in flight

Is the fight, for space

For the right, to mate

With the best egg layer of the season.

Thrashing, clashing time and again,

Lashing left and right

In squawking, pecking refrain!

Glossy blue black, a flash, of bright orange!

Noisy and primitive
fighting to live!
Ending quickly, predictably in defeat and retreat
From the newcomer.

The dowdy brown hen passively accepts the victor.
Without resistance.

Each year this repeating ritual occurs.
An avian formality.
For Turdus Merula mates for life!
And makes its home, similarly – when it can,
In the familiarity of the same, safe garden space
It has used before.

The blackbird;
A rowdy primeval mini beast.
The wolf in sheep's clothing of garden birds.

Driven. Defensive
Against pesky, pecky freeloading young whippersnappers,
Who,
Attempt to take without effort or right,
Like Cuckoo,
What belongs to another

Dream

Delicate. Dancing dandelions over green.
                        Yellow Stars
That float, gleam;
Sway, below the cloudless
                    blue sky of a July afternoon.

Daisies stretch and strain to reply
Whilst butterflies, frolic and flutter
Speedily together
                    Above them.

The breeze whispers to ears that wait
For fay fairies to be imagined;
                    in minds that seek escape
From earthly reality to fairy tales and dragons.

Seeking diversion from
                    Dismal   despondencies
of gloom and doom, and a world known to be
                    spinning into oblivion.

In this dying planet we call Earth – our home.
Where is the Whole Eden that was?
Reduced to single plots, preserved by the few?
Interspersed by concrete and treeless plains?
Decimated, by the biped primitive that names
itself as human and

                            Higher than the Apes.

Taking all and giving too little, too late,
Trickles

                            to save a world.

And so
We sit, and wait.

                            In our small plots.

Jewels

No gold
or silver spoon to start.
No coins that bulge the purse, no trinkets, tokens
heartfelt baubles chosen.
These gestures others hold dear.
Others who have less
granted.

This mind has riches a-plenty
beyond compare,
with priceless tag
a wealth of joy
Seemingly worthless to the materialist,
who deals only in things
and spends.
Take your coins – stash them away – keep them forever and a day.
Then what?

To find
wealth in your mind –
is richness.

To find
Talent.
Sing out,
Paint your world.
Fingers play!
Throughout a long,
otherwise tedious day.

Look within.
freedom to say
content am I with my words, my colours, my tunes
that lure you to listen, see and
Be,
happy
for a moment?

No value, yet priceless –
this one life lived
in which words now fly free,
Unexpectedly,
At any time of the day or night forcing me
to stop and take note of seemingly, meaningless babbling
In my head.

In my head

A precious store of jewels in sentences unthought of,

which drop, unbidden into the field of my vacant hidden thinking

and drip out on to the paper from the pencil point,

as if from a leaking tap.

If there is a God – a celestial will to which we bend or are bent by –

Then this beneficence

Is overwhelming.

These riches –

unseen.

From childhood

known.

In my own control.

Growing.

Even now

As the days pound on.

A Path to Peace

As the cat licks her paws,
Ears and head
Poised.
Soft noise,
Purring,
soothing.

Are you listening?
Seeing the peace in this moment
In your country garden home?
While glistening drops of rain,
trickle lazily down the pane,
Are you feeling unburdened?
Whilst morning rain
falls,
And all,
Wait quietly.

The clock ticks on the mantel piece.
The smell of bread from the stove.

We, capsule-like, awake
And wait, for day to wake
Upon us
And break,
Our early morning reverie –
This peace of non-activity.

Elsewhere,
In this world of contrasts,
"The bombs were less last night."
Yet now the siren calls,
"Head underground!
Run for your life."

Take your cat – no purring here.
The peace of death is all that you may hear,
You can expect.
This day.

The kettle falls from the fire.
The pictures from the walls.
Yet rays of hope
For Peace,
Seep still.

It sits in minds
That crave it,
However tangled,
waiting to be resurrected
by a memory, a place,
a sound, sight or gesture.
Or a sacred space.

However hopeless
And sad the plight might seem.
We reach and find our own path to Peace.
It creeps, ivy-like
And sits, within us.

The Working Horse

Together, eye to eye.
From the side,
head on.
For a short while, lingering.
Dark brown I saw in his eyes.
Warm, kind, wise.
Recognition.
Understanding, so deep
it could not be explained,
and none should try
to fathom the abyss, or depth of it.

Make no precocious assumption,
By human ignorance of it –
This natural connection of **Two.**
Two,
Who, just happen to be
Here – at the same time.
Once mutually dependent.

And I saw and felt a sort of sadness in his eyes
And in myself,
That I, would have liked, to remove.

He allowed me to touch him, tentative fingers on velveteen.

No alarm or resentment.

Welcoming. Expected.

All the time looking – eye to eye -

His - deep brown. Large.

Mine - bluey green. Small.

Old friends – respecting, recognising each other.

Encounters resurfaced!

Often as a child I have done this.

Looked into the eyes of other such working horses.

Ridden in all weathers,

Ploughing the fields, Together.

Head lowered,

Plodding heavily

Along the part frozen furrows,

In biting cold fen winds.

Tucking my hands under his neck collar to keep them warm.

Ah! but then came the tractor.

Mechanisation.

Out to grass

No usefulness

A curiosity– parades, galas, obstacle courses.

Oh, for the Charge! at the end of the day.
To drive the carriage again under blue skies
galloping along empty country lanes.
Reins, in hand,
White creamy froth, plumes of sweat
Rising, flying and clumping,
Landing cloudlike,
Lathering face
As we chase
Through the high-hedged, hidden Droves.

Hearts pounding in tandem!
Shoes clanking,
Drumming steadily
A musical, energetic thumping rhythm on the road.
Muscles rippling,
Finding joy,
Heading home
In eagerness.
Together.

www.ingramcontent.com/pod-product-compliance
Lightning Source LLC
Chambersburg PA
CBHW052210110526
44591CB00012B/2152